Setting Limits: Promoting Positive Parenting

The PACTS series: *Parent, Adolescent and Child Training Skills*

1. Assessing Children in Need and Their Parents
2. ABC of Behavioural Methods
3. Bonding: Infantile and Parental Attachments
4. Coping with Children's Feeding Problems and Bedtime Battles
5. Toilet Training, Bedwetting and Soiling
6. Social Skills Training for Children
7. Setting Limits: Promoting Positive Parenting
8. Feuding and Fighting
9. Banishing Bad Behaviour: Helping Parents Cope with a Child's Conduct Disorder
10. Supporting Bereaved and Dying Children and Their Parents
11. Separation and Divorce
12. Post-Traumatic Stress Disorder in Children

Setting Limits: Promoting Positive Parenting

by
Martin Herbert

First published in 1996 by BPS Books (The British Psychological Society), St Andrews House, 48 Princess Road East, Leicester LE1 7DR, UK.

A catalogue record for this book is available from the British Library.

ISBN 1 85433 189 2

Typeset by Ralph Footring, Derby.

Printed in Great Britain by Stanley L. Hunt Printers Ltd., Rushden, Northants.

Contents

Setting limits: promoting positive parenting

Introduction

Aims

The aim of this guide is to help practitioners deal with the issue of positive discipline when consulted by parents whose children are proving difficult to manage.

Objectives

The objective of this guide is to provide practitioners with information and skills to help parents (and other caregivers) to strike a balance between being too permissive and too restrictive. This involves looking at:

- setting fair, firm limits;
- communicating reasonable and appropriate rules;
- giving clear, courteous but assertive instructions and commands;
- praising and encouraging co-operation;
- applying consistent consequences to misbehaviour.

Behavioural boundaries or limits are the messages that convey parents' rules and expectations to the child. They also define the balance of power and authority in family relationships and constitute a crucial element in child-rearing.

A variety of studies tell us that children whose parents set firm limits for them grow up with more self-esteem and confidence than those who are allowed to get away with behaving in any way they like. It is important, however, to give youngsters some freedom of choice *within reasonable limits*. Research also tells us that well-adjusted children tend to have parents who are warm, nurturant, supportive, reasonably controlling and also have high expectations. Firm control is associated with independence in the child, provided that the control is not restrictive of his/her opportunities to experiment and be spontaneous (see Herbert, 1974; 1991).

Let us take an example of a child who fails to recognize limits. The words are those of a worried mother, talking about her four-year-old son, Robert.

> By the time his sister Ann was born, Robert had got used to being the king-pin in the family. He liked all the attention that illness brought him, enjoyed the privileges of being an only child, and he was beginning to learn the art of getting his own way in a sly manner. He was intensely jealous of the new baby. Feeding times with Ann were a nightmare with Robert taking advantage of my immobility to throw tantrums, be disobedient, and to be aggressive towards me and Ann. He couldn't bear her to be held close, and was so spiteful I daren't leave him alone with her even for a few seconds. He threw things into her cot, pulled, poked and scratched. Occasionally he tried to tip the cot over.

As time went by, Robert developed into a small despot. He became increasingly aggressive, developed a high degree of wilfulness, clung like a limpet, was insecure and anxious, and incessantly disobedient. However, given that Robert's behaviours – insecurity and tantrums, defiance, aggressiveness, and so on – are displayed by *most* children, can they actually be called abnormal or problematic?

There is no clear distinction between the characteristics of problem children and other children. The differences are all relative; there are no *absolute* symptoms of psychological maladjustment in children. Most children are difficult at times, and parents tend to get the blame. 'There are no problem children, only problem parents' is a simplistic and misleading aphorism, reflected in the following couplet:

> Come listen now to the good old days when children, strange to tell,
> Were seen not heard, led a simple life, in short, were brought up well.

This is not, as might be thought, a present-day grandmother bemoaning the passing of strict child-rearing practices and well-behaved children. The lines are from Aristophanes, and date back to the fifth century BC. Mind you, even this is a *relatively* contemporary statement; an inscription discovered and attributed to an Egyptian priest voices the complaint – some 6,000 years ago – that 'our earth is degenerate; children no longer obey their parents'. Nothing much changes!

Part I: Discipline

Positive discipline

This guide advocates a style of positive discipline to discuss and debate with parents; one that provides an alternative to the counter-productive extremes of authoritarian punishment and *laissez-faire* permissiveness. The assumption here is that effective discipline takes into account the child's (or adolescent's) *emotional* life, and their agendas – the developmental tasks that confront and challenge them at different stages in their growing up. If we think of discipline as a means to an end, as guidance, then the best time to start is from the very beginning, by setting an example that derives its influence from a relationship of respect, trust and affection.

Discipline is, among other things, about setting limits. This is one of the hardest tasks for parents, especially when it comes to toddlers and teenagers whose tasks include finding out about life and doing things *for themselves!* Another difficulty concerns tactics or methods: the issue of *how* to discipline. There are different approaches and different philosophies associated with the word 'discipline'. For many people discipline is uncomfortably equated with the words 'punishment' and 'repression', with the result that parents sometimes become tentative and inconsistent in disciplining their children for fear of seeming old-fashioned, reactionary or overly intrusive. Care and control are the issues over which the allegedly 'terrible teens' provide such a daunting challenge, and adolescents often accuse their hapless parents of being Victorian and fuddy duddy. The following statement could well have come from a staid Victorian:

> The children now love luxury. They have bad manners, contempt for authority, they show disrespect to their elders and love to chat in places of exercise. They no longer get up when their elders enter the room. They contradict parents, chatter before company, gobble up dainties at the table, cross their legs and are tyrants over their teachers.

This querulous voice belongs to Socrates. Apparently fourth-century teachers, like their modern-day counterparts, had to cope with disruptive pupils. Yet the breakdown in discipline is seen as a relatively contemporary phenomenon and is blamed for many present-day problems.

Young parents are subject to many warnings about the dangers of spoiling their offspring, thus encouraging bad habits and indiscipline. That voice of Socrates, coming to us over the centuries, reminds us that the older generation has always looked askance at the lack of discipline, obedience and respect among the young. The reasons are not hard to find. Obedience to rules, whether they are laid down by convention, codified in laws, or hidden in our consciences, is a prerequisite for social living. All parents and teachers are beset at one time or another by disobedient children. But there is *disobedience* and there is *serious defiance*. Parents and teachers are more sensitive to the breaking of certain kinds of rules than they are to the breaking of others, particularly those that involve what might be called moral rules. It is when children lie, steal, cheat or hurt others by their aggression that parents get most perturbed.

When there are few limits

Of course, there is difficult behaviour and there is *really* difficult behaviour. According to the American Psychiatric Association's classification (APA, 1993) of childhood disorder (DSM-IV Criteria), Oppositional Defiant Disorder (ODD) is very much to do with the failure of the child to recognize and/or comply with limits to his/her behaviour. The diagnosis of ODD requires a pattern of negativistic, hostile, and defiant behaviour lasting at least six months, during which four of the following are present:

- often loses temper;
- often argues with adults;
- often deliberately does things that annoy other people;
- often blames others for his/her mistakes;
- is often touchy or easily annoyed;
- is often angry and resentful; and
- is often vindictive.

Melinda (reported in Webster-Stratton and Herbert, 1994) showed all the signs of ODD at six years of age.

> She screams and tantrums when she fails to get her own way at school. She also behaves impulsively and can be hyperactive in the classroom. Her teachers have threatened to expel her from kindergarten for these behaviours. Her mother reports that at home Melinda throws chairs

> and threatens her with knives. She whines incessantly to get what she wants and refuses to brush her teeth, to get dressed, or to go to bed. Her mother feels unable to go out in public with Melinda because of her emotional outbursts. She reports that every request involves a series of intensive negotiations and cajoling. The mother says Melinda has been difficult since she was eight months old. She reports feeling exhausted and trapped, isolated from other adults by her situation and unable to invite friends over socially. She feels that her daughter 'blackmails' both her parents and her teachers to get what she wants by her aggressive outbursts, which sometimes last for over an hour.

'Spoiling' children

The words of Aristophanes have a particularly poignant resonance for parents in the light of contemporary uncertainties about child rearing. Young mothers in particular are subjected to many warnings about the dangers of spoiling their offspring, thus encouraging bad habits and indiscipline. Parents are pulled in two directions; if they are too permissive, the child will become (it is said) an overly dependent 'satellite' to his/her parents or a self-centred, unpopular and wilful tyrant. But if they are too restrictive, authoritarian and punitive, their discipline will produce slavish conformity and a neurotic, submissive nonentity.

Can one really spoil a baby by allowing him/her to display his/her dependency needs, for example, crying to be picked up? Among the things s/he needs in abundance are human attention, stimulation and intimate company. The mother who has an accepting and tolerant attitude towards dependent behaviour will tend to be responsive to her baby's crying, picking up the baby fairly promptly. Such responsiveness is *not* associated with a later 'clinging' type of dependency in children (see Herbert, 1991, for a discussion of the assessment and implications of parental responsiveness).

The trouble with dependency needs is that every child has savoured the delights of being cared for, as even the most reluctant parent has to minister to certain of his/her child's wants. So the child knows what it is missing and craves for more, especially if s/he is not specifically discouraged by punishment. This is where dependency training differs from training in such matters as sex and aggression. Children are seldom knowingly encouraged, that is to say rewarded, for sexual or aggressive behaviour.

Conformity

A child can be too submissive to authority, be it the coercive influence of the individual or the group. Does s/he stick up for her/his own rights or point of view, or meekly give in to the wishes and attitudes of others? Hopefully, the child will learn to discriminate between the desirability or undesirability of people, and between particular demands and values. However, in return for absolute obedience, some parents will overindulge their children's every whim in an attempt to prolong their childhood and keep them tied to the parental apron strings.

The 'brat syndrome'

Children brought up in this way are quite likely to turn out to be 'lovable little tyrants' in mum's and dad's eyes, but 'spoiled brats' in the view of others. Outsiders see an exploitive character using every device – charm, wheedling, coaxing, and bullying – in order to get his/her own way. Unless this is stemmed by reality experiences, the child may continue to play the part of the beloved tyrant into adult life, encouraged by ever-responding parents. This incessant babying might leave the *enfant terrible* with a permanent illusion of omnipotence.

Part II: Socialization

One of the main objectives of socialization is the preparation of children for their future. Social development is a life process founded upon the paradox that we are both *social* and *individual* creatures. We associate with others in a multitude of ways, but ultimately stand alone in the world.

Assimilation and accommodation

The basic biological impetus of all living beings to adapt, by modifying the self and the environment, is reflected in two interrelated processes. **Assimilation** involves a person's adjustment of the environment to him/herself, and represents the individual's use of his/her environment as s/he perceives it. **Accommodation** is the converse of assimilation and involves the impact on the individual of the actual environment itself. To accommodate is to perceive and to incorporate the experience provided by the environment as it actually is.

One might say that mature social development is the achievement of a balance between assimilation and accommodation, between one's self-centred needs and an altruistic concern for others. Another way of putting this is that healthy personality development and satisfactory social relationships can be described in terms of a balance between the child's need to make demands on others, and his/her ability to recognize the demands which others ask of him/her.

This process begins during the first year of life, a year that is foundational but *not* irreversible for the child's development. Within the space of 365 days, such momentous events take place, that by her/his first birthday, the previously asocial newborn could be said to have well and truly joined the human race.

Discipline becomes a very real issue in the child's second year of life, although the foundations for good disciplinary practices should have been laid down much earlier by the loving, responsive care provided and the gradual establishment of routines. Notions of right and wrong, a code of behaviour, a set of attitudes and values, the ability to see the other person's point of view – all of the basic qualities which make an individual into a socialized personality – are nurtured in the first instance by parents.

The importance of trust

It could be said that the first and most important step in the socialization of the child occurs when s/he develops a *willingness* to do as s/he is told. The child's relationship of trust and affection with parents is critical because it ensures that the child is essentially on the same side as those who are teaching the social and moral lessons of life. The child identifies with her/his parents and is, therefore, more likely to internalize the values and rules being taught. Socialization involves discipline, something that is not always welcome to children. However, children who get their own way all the time can interpret such *laissez-faire* permissiveness as indifference; they feel that nothing they do is important enough for their parents to bother about (see Herbert, 1974; 1989; 1991 for a review of the evidence).

Discipline

Mothers and fathers need to be firm and unbending at times, tough as well as lovingly tender, and yet also flexible at crucial moments. They also need to know when to move from one mode to the other. This blend fits the recommendations of child-rearing specialists who are concerned with fostering approaches and attitudes which result in children who are socially responsible and outgoing, friendly, competent, creative, reasonably independent and self-assertive.

The balance is perhaps best illustrated in the philosophy of what is called the 'authoritative parent'. These parents attempt to direct their child's activities in a rational manner determined by the issues involved in particular disciplinary situations. They encourage verbal give-and-take, and share with the child the reasoning behind their policy. They value both the child's self-expression and his/her respect for authority, work and the like. The evidence, from the research literature on parenting, according to Diana Baumrind (1971), points to a synthesis and balancing of strongly opposing forces of tradition and innovation, divergence and convergence (that is, unconventional vs. conventional thinking), accommodation and assimilation, co-operation and independent expression, tolerance and principled intractability.

This can be illustrated in the case of the mother who appreciates both independent self-will and disciplined conformity. She exerts firm control at those points where she and her child disagree in viewpoint, but does not hem the child in with restrictions. She recognizes her own special rights as an adult, but also recognizes the child's individual interests and special ways. She affirms the child's present qualities, but also sets standards for future conduct using reason as well as power to achieve her objectives. Her decisions are not based solely on the consensus of the group or on the individual child's desires, but she also does not regard herself as infallible or divinely inspired.

Three approaches to discipline

The philosophy that might underlie approaches to discipline is the subject of Robert MacKenzie's 1993 book *Setting Limits*. He suggests that most parents use disciplinary methods based on three basic approaches to training: the **democratic**, **permissive** and **authoritarian** (punitive/autocratic) approaches. Each approach is thought to teach the child or adolescent a different set of lessons about co-operation, responsibility and expectations about what is acceptable or unacceptable behaviour. The approaches are summarized in *Table 1*.

Table 1: Three approaches to discipline

Disciplinary approach	Limits	Methods of problem-solving
Democratic	Freedom within limits	Through co-operation and accountability
Permissive	Freedom without limits	By persuasion
Authoritarian	Limits without freedom	By force

Democratic parenting

MacKenzie describes the democratic approach as follows.

Parents' beliefs

- Children are capable of solving problems on their own.
- Children should be given choices and allowed to learn from the consequences of their choices.
- Encouragement is an effective way to motivate co-operation.

Power and control

- Children are given only as much power and control as they can handle responsibly.

Problem-solving process

- Co-operative.
- Win–win (child *and* parent win).
- Based on mutual respect.
- Children are active participants in the problem-solving process.

What children learn

- Responsibility.
- Co-operation.
- Children should be given choices and allowed to learn from the consequences of their choices.
- Encouragement is an effective way to motivate co-operation.

Permissive parenting

Permissiveness has become an emotive word in our vocabulary. When adults wring their hands and bemoan the 'permissive society', they forget that they are passing judgement on themselves; they carried out the socialization of the youngsters they now deprecate. The word 'permissiveness' has a technical meaning (see following), and also a popular meaning, with the main connotation of 'lax discipline'. It is misleading to use the term without knowing what is going on within the family. A child who is permitted to do pretty well what s/he likes against a background of 'couldn't-care-less' or hostile attitudes from parents, is very different from the child who is given this freedom against a background of parental support and love.

The word 'permissiveness' is sometimes used as if it defined the extreme end of the freedom dimension – a licence for a child to do whatever s/he wishes. Yet there are all kinds of degrees of permitted freedoms. MacKenzie (1993) summarizes the permissive approach as follows.

Parents' beliefs

- Children will co-operate when they understand that co-operation is the right thing to do.
- My job is to serve my children and keep them happy.
  Consequences that upset my children cannot be effective.

Power and control

- All for children.

Problem-solving process

- Problem-solving by persuasion.
- Win–lose (children win).
- Parents do most of the problem-solving.

What children learn

- 'Rules are for others, not me. I do as I wish'.
- Parents serve children.
- Parents are responsible for solving children's problems.
- Dependency, disrespect, self-centredness.

How children respond

- Limit testing.
- Challenge and defy rules and authority.

- Ignore and tune out words.
- Wear parents down with words.

Authoritarian parenting

The authoritarian parent attempts to shape, control and assess the behaviour and attitudes of their child according to a set standard of conduct (usually an absolute standard) motivated by ideological (children are one's property; they have to obey) or theological considerations, such as religious dogma about morals, and formulated by a higher authority (God or the Church). S/he values obedience as a virtue and favours punitive, forceful measures to curb self-will at those points where the child's actions or beliefs conflict with what s/he thinks is the right conduct. Children should be indoctrinated with such values as respect for authority, respect for work, and respect for the preservation of traditional order. Such parents do not encourage verbal give and take, believing that the child should accept his/her word for what is right. MacKenzie summarizes the authoritarian approach as follows.

Parents' beliefs

- If it doesn't hurt, children won't learn.

Power and control

- All for parents.

Problem-solving process

- Problem-solving by force.
- Adversarial.
- Win–lose (parents win).
- Parents do all the problem-solving and make all the decisions.
- Parents direct and control the process.

What children learn

- Parents are responsible for solving children's problems.
- Hurtful methods of communication and problem-solving.

How children respond

- Anger, stubbornness.
- Revenge, rebellion.
- Withdrawal, fearful submission.

Remember: these are generalities; caricatures, but recognizable ones. Generally, there are various shades of grey, nuances and variations in these broad disciplinary orientations.

The golden mean

Research into child-rearing techniques suggests that there is a happy medium – a golden mean – but this is not always easy to achieve in practice. The extremes of permissiveness and restrictiveness entail risks. For example, there is evidence to suggest that strict, autocratic adult domination and restrictiveness may indeed produce a conforming child, but will handicap his/her initiative (Herbert, 1974). Such a child may turn out to be rather passive, colourless, unimaginative and incurious, and burdened, in addition, with shyness and a sense of inadequacy. The children of domineering parents usually lack self-reliance and the ability to cope realistically with their problems, and later on may fail (or be slow) to accept adult responsibilities. They are apt to be submissive and obedient, and to withdraw from situations they find difficult.

The child with warm, democratic parents is brought up and trained mainly through love, has good models to identify with and imitate, is given reasons for actions and rules, and the opportunity to learn for her/himself (by trial and error) how his/her actions affect others and themselves. A variety of studies tell us that well-adjusted children tend to have parents who are warm, nurturant, supportive, reasonably controlling and they also have high expectations. Firm control is associated with independence in the child, provided that the control is not restrictive of his/her opportunities to experiment and be spontaneous (see Herbert, 1974; 1989).

Healthy personality development and the formation of satisfactory social relationships can be described as the results of a balance between the child's need to make demands on others, and their ability to recognize the demands which others make on them. A blend of limit-setting and a warm, encouraging and accepting attitude on the part of the parents is perhaps best illustrated in the so-called 'democratic' or 'authoritative' parent.

Part III: Disciplinary tactics

Teaching parents to praise

Rules or statements about expected behaviour are not sufficient for motivating behaviour; the only way a child learns to engage in a particular behaviour is by having that behaviour reinforced. A rule or statement which is not reinforced when those expectations are met will be without long-term effect. Some parents do not believe they should have to praise their children for everyday behaviours, while others do not know how or when to give praise and encouragement. Perhaps they themselves received little praise from their own parents when they were young. Unaccustomed to hearing praise, they tend not to notice praiseworthy child behaviours when they do occur.

Parents can be taught to respond to positive behaviours and to praise them. Here are the major points to emphasize with parents when you are discussing their child's behaviour:

- Make praise contingent on behaviour.
- Praise immediately.
- Give labelled and specific praise.
- Give positive praise, without qualifiers or sarcasm.
- Praise with smiles, eye contact, and enthusiasm as well as with words.
- Give pats, hugs, and kisses along with verbal praise.
- Catch the child whenever s/he is being good – don't save praise for perfect behaviour only.
- Use praise consistently whenever you see the positive behaviour you want to encourage.
- Praise in front of other people.
- Increase praise for difficult children.
- Show the child how to praise him/herself for appropriate behaviour.

Some people give praise and then, without realizing it, undermine it by being sarcastic or combining it with a punishing remark. This is one of the most disruptive things a parent can do.

Note: for some oppositional and challenging children, parental praise is initially not enough reinforcement to reverse difficult problem behaviour. However, a tangible reward could be used by parents to provide the added incentive necessary for a child to achieve a particular goal. A tangible reward is something concrete, such as a special treat, additional privileges or a favourite activity. Tangible rewards can be used to encourage such positive behaviours in children as playing co-operatively with siblings, learning how to get dressed, getting ready for school on time, completing homework, cleaning up their room, and so on. When the parents are using tangible rewards to motivate children to learn something new, you will need to stress the importance of their continuing to provide social rewards (that is, attention and praise) as well. The impact is much greater when both types of rewards are combined.

Reward systems (or *operant programmes*) will be effective only if parents:

- define the desired behaviour clearly;
- choose effective rewards (that is, rewards that the child will find sufficiently reinforcing);
- set consistent limits concerning which behaviours will receive rewards;
- make the programme simple and fun;
- make the steps small;
- monitor the charts carefully (see examples in *Appendices I* and *II* at the back of this booklet);
- follow through with the rewards immediately;
- avoid mixing rewards with punishment;
- gradually replace rewards with social approval;
- revise the programme as the behaviours and rewards change.

While reward programmes may seem simple, there are many pitfalls to be avoided if they are to be effective. You as the therapist will need to spend time reviewing charts and trouble-shooting knotty problems that arise as parents begin these programmes (see Herbert, 1987; Webster-Stratton and Herbert, 1994). Charts are provided in *Appendices I* and *II*.

Limit-setting

Once you have taught parents the importance of using play, praise, and rewards for promoting more appropriate behaviours in their children, you can help them learn how to decrease inappropriate behaviour through effective limit-setting. Indeed, research indicates that families who have few clearly communicated standards or rules are more likely to have children who misbehave.

However, while clear limit-setting is essential in helping children behave more appropriately, it is also important to remember that all children will test their parents' rules and standards. Research shows that normal children fail to comply with their parents' requests about one-third of the time. Young children will argue, scream, or throw temper tantrums when a toy is taken away or a desired activity prohibited. School-age children, too, will argue or protest when barred from something they want. This is normal behaviour, and an irritating but healthy expression of a child's need for independence and autonomy.

This is all very well in the case of the normal child, but the conduct-disordered child differs in that s/he is refusing to comply with a parent's requests about two-thirds of the time – that is, the parent is engaged in a power struggle with the child for the majority of the time. This high rate of noncompliance makes it very difficult for parents to socialize their children adequately, and firm limits become even more essential (see *Figure 1*).

Teaching parents to use effective 'time-out' skills

In the initial stages of intervention, the main focus is to teach the parents the importance of providing the child with ongoing and regular communication and expression of parental love, support, and understanding. Next, teach parents how to provide clear limits and consequences for their children's misbehaviour. Many parents have tried spanking, lecturing, criticism, and expressions of disapproval when their children are aggressive and noncompliant. These are ineffective methods of discipline and usually parents of aggressive children find themselves spiralling into more and more spanking and yelling in order to get their children to respond. In fact, nagging, criticizing, hitting, shouting, or even reasoning with children while they misbehave are forms of parental attention and therefore actually reinforce the particular misbehaviour; they result in children learning to nag, criticize, hit, shout, or argue in response to their parents.

Time-out can be taught to parents for use with high-intensity problems, such as fighting, defiance, hitting, and destructive behaviour. Time-out is actually an extreme form of parental ignoring in which children are removed for a brief period from all sources of positive reinforcement, especially adult attention.

	Firm limits	Soft limits
Characteristics	Stated in clear, direct, concrete behavioural terms.	Stated in unclear terms, or as 'mixed messages'.
	Words supported by actions.	Actions do not support intended rule.
	Compliance expected and required.	Compliance optional; not required.
	Provides information needed to make acceptable choices and co-operate.	Does not provide information needed to make acceptable choices.
	Provides accountability	Lacks accountability.
Predictable outcomes	Co-operation.	Resistance.
	Decreased limit testing.	Increased limit testing.
	Clear understanding of rules and expectations.	Escalating misbehaviour, power struggles.
	Regard parents' words seriously.	Ignore and tune out parents' words.
Children learn	'No' means 'No'.	'No' means 'Yes', 'Some times' or 'Maybe'.
	'I'm expected and required to follow the rules'.	'I'm not expected to follow the rules'.
	'Rules apply to me like everyone else'.	'Rules are for others, not me'.
	'I am responsible for my own behaviour'.	'I make my own rules and do what I want'.
	Adults mean what they say.	'Adults don't mean what they say'.
		'Adults are responsible for my behaviour'.

Figure 1: Comparison of firm and soft limits (adapted from MacKenzie, 1993)

When introducing the method, do encourage the parents to persevere. Remind them that some behaviours change only slowly. If they take the line of least resistance, 'giving-in' on the odd occasion ('Just this once'), they won't be back to square one; it will be square minus one! They will actually make things worse for themselves. Tell them not to be discouraged if things get worse before they get better. If they remove the old reinforcers, the child may well work harder (say by escalating the screaming) to get them back.

Points to emphasize to parents

- Don't threaten time-out unless you are prepared to follow through.
- Give three to five-minutes time-outs with repeats if the child is refusing to comply with a reasonable command.
- Ignore the child while in time-out.
- Be prepared for his/her testing your resolve and consistency.
- Hold children responsible for messes in time-out.
- Support a partner's use of time-out.
- Carefully limit the number of behaviours for which time-out is used.
- Don't rely exclusively on time-out – combine it with other techniques, such as ignoring, logical consequences, and problem-solving.
- Expect repeated learning trials.
- Use nonviolent approaches such as loss of privileges as back-up to time-out.
- Use personal time-out to relax and refuel your energy.
- Be polite.
- Build up a 'bank account' with praise, love and support.

Teaching parents to use response–cost

If a child does something, and as a result of, or following, this action something unrewarding – a penalty – happens to him/her, then s/he will be less likely to do that thing again in the future. A cost (fine, loss of privilege) for behaving in that way means s/he is less likely to behave in that way again. For example, if the parent says something like, 'John, since you are throwing your dinner about, you've clearly had enough' and removes his plate each time food-throwing happens, John will be less likely to throw food again.

A child is likely to learn to behave positively (for example, not breaking a toy) in order to avoid a punishment (such as having it removed altogether). A warning of the penalty becomes enough of a reminder. The technical term for doing more of something to avoid a penalty is *negative reinforcement*.

Some examples of negative reinforcement

If Nisha keeps getting down from the table, she can be told that next time she gets down the meal will be over for her. No attempt should be made to persuade her to eat, and no biscuits or snacks given before the next regular meal.

If Wayne demands (screams) to go to the swings, his parents can decide what *they* think is appropriate – *and stick to it*. They might caution him that he will not be able to play with his computer game that evening if he continues to tantrum. His tantrums are likely to die away when he learns that they do not result in either his getting his own way, or in his gaining attention. Nor does he want his playtime on the computer curtailed. (**Note:** he must believe his parents' warnings.)

If Darrell runs all over the house on returning from playgroup, he can be told that a regular event, which it is known that he likes, such as 10 minutes of doing a jigsaw with Mum, will be starting in one minute. This should only be 'on offer' for one minute, so that he learns that things he likes need a quick, co-operative reaction from him.

Teaching parents about natural and logical consequences

One of the most important and difficult tasks for parents of oppositional children is to help their children become more independent and responsible. The therapist can help parents foster their children's decision-making, sense of responsibility, and ability to learn from mistakes through the use of natural and logical consequences. A *natural consequence* is whatever would result from a child's action or inaction in the absence of adult intervention. For instance, if Ryan slept in or refused to go on the school bus, the natural consequence would be that he would have to walk to school. If Caitlin did not want to wear her coat, then she would get cold. In these examples, the children learn from experiencing the direct consequences of their own decisions and thus they are not protected from the possibility of an undesirable outcome of their behaviour by their parents' commands. A *logical consequence*, on the other hand, is designed by the parent; 'punishment to fit the crime'. A logical consequence for a youngster who broke a neighbour's window would be to do chores in order to make up the cost of the replacement. A logical consequence for stealing would be to take the object back to the store, apologize to the store owner, and do an extra chore or lose a privilege. In other words, when parents use this technique, they hold children accountable for their mistakes by helping them make up for the error in some way.

In contrast to ignoring or time-out, natural and logical consequences teach children to be more responsible. These strategies are most effective for recurring problems where parents are able to decide ahead of time how they will follow through in the event that the misbehaviour occurs.

These are the main points to emphasize to parents:

- Make consequences immediate.
- Make consequences age-appropriate.
- Make consequences nonpunitive.
- Use consequences that are brief and to the point.
- Involve the child whenever possible.
- Be friendly and positive.
- Give the child a choice of consequences ahead of time.
- Be sure parents can live with the consequences they have set up.
- Quickly offer new learning opportunities to be successful.

References

American Psychiatric Association (1993). *Diagnostic and Statistical Manual of Mental Disorders*, 4th edn (DSM IV). Washington, D.C.: American Psychiatric Association.

Baumrind, D. (1971). Current patterns of parental authority. *Developmental Psychology Monographs, 4, (1), Part 2*, 1–103.

Herbert, M. (1974). *Emotional Problems of Development in Children*. London: Academic Press.

Herbert, M. (1987). *Behavioural Treatment of Children with Problems: A practice manual*. London: Academic Press.

Herbert, M. (1989). *Discipline: A positive guide for parents*. Oxford: Basil Blackwell.

Herbert, M. (1991). *Clinical Child Psychology: Social learning, development and behaviour.* Chichester: Wiley.

MacKenzie, R. J. (1993). *Setting Limits*. Rocklin, C.A.: Prima Publishing.

Webster-Stratton, C. and Herbert, M. (1994). *Troubled Families: Problem children*. Chichester: John Wiley.

Further reading

Herbert, M. (1991). *Child Care and the Family.* Windsor: NFER-Nelson. This is a client management resource pack.

Herbert, M. (1993). *Working with Children and the Children Act*. Leicester: BPS Books (The British Psychological Society).

Appendix I: Frequency Chart

Child's name:
Date:
Week no.:

Target behaviours:
1. ____________________
2. ____________________
3. ____________________

	Monday	*Tuesday*	*Wednes-day*	*Thurs-day*	*Friday*	*Saturday*	*Sunday*
6–8 a.m.							
8–10 a.m.							
10–12 a.m.							
12–2 p.m.							
2–4 p.m.							
4–6 p.m.							
6–8 p.m.							
8–10 p.m.							
10–12 p.m.							
12–2 a.m.							
2–4 a.m.							
4–6 a.m.							

Appendix II: ABC Record

Child's name:
Child's age:
Date:

Behaviour being recorded:

Date and time	*Antecedent:* what happened beforehand?	*Behaviour:* what did your child do?	*Consequences:* what was the end result? (i) What did you do (e.g. ignore, argue, scold, smack, etc.)? (ii) How did s/he react?	Describe your feelings

Hints for Parents 1: Setting limits

The joys of parents are secret, and so are their griefs
(Francis Bacon, 1597)

Many of the 'griefs' referred to by Francis Bacon come to parents in the course of disciplinary encounters with their children. Some parents feel too ashamed to admit the difficulties they are having with their children, and thus their grief often remains secret. The failure to set limits on children's impulses, wants and actions, is the source of much of the misery in today's parent–child relationships. Children have rights, but so do you, the parents, and most particularly, mothers!

Setting down limits

The ideal balance is a compromise between sometimes incompatible mutual demands, and a style of life which maximizes the mutually rewarding possibilities of the parent–child relationship. This 'golden mean', if it is achieved, is established over a long period of time, during the process of socialization (the process of acquiring the knowledge, values, language and social skills which enable an individual to be integrated into their society). It begins with obedience training.

Not surprisingly, children are likely to complain and compare their lot with other children when limits are set down and insisted on. However, there is clear evidence to show that children realize that their parents are firm *because they care*. Children know, deep down, that they cannot cope alone. They need to know someone has charge of their lives so that they can learn about, and experiment with, life from a safe base.

Children who get their own way all the time interpret such permissiveness as indifference; they feel nothing they do is important enough for their parents to bother about. If you have to cope with tantrums, recriminations and sulks, grit your teeth, take heart and take the long view. Remain solid and secure; it may cost you a grey hair or two, but it will pay off in the long term.

Hints for Parents 2: Coping with your child's behaviour

Colour-coding behaviours

You could think of your child's behaviour as falling into three colour codes: green, amber and red.

- **Green** is the 'go ahead' code for the type of behaviour you want from your children, the actions you always remember to praise and encourage. If you use the green code consistently, this behaviour should be well established by the time they go to school.
- **Amber** is for 'caution' behaviour, which you don't encourage but tolerate because your child is still learning and making mistakes. This includes behaviour such as hurling toys across the room in a moment of fury. Any sort of stress, such as moving house, illness or upset in the family, may cause the child to take a temporary step backwards in behaviour. Be understanding if your child suddenly starts wetting the bed or crying for attention following a bad dream in the night, a major change in routines or a distressing life event, such as a bereavement.
- **Red** is definite 'stop' (No! No!) behaviour which needs to be curbed as soon as possible, such as running into the road.

Any limits set should be for the child's safety, well-being and development; **do not make up rules for the sake of having rules**. Keep them to essentials. It is crucial to ensure that the child knows exactly what they are and what is expected of him/her. Here is a checklist:

- Are your rules simple?
- Are your rules fair?
- Does your child understand them?
- Does your child know what will happen if s/he breaks them?
- Are the rules applied fairly and consistently?

The priorities must be appropriate to the child; rules for older children and teenagers will, of course, be different than those for toddlers.

Being firm

Your difficulty may be that you find it hard to be really firm with your child and this really does cause a lot of people difficulties. If your child has got into the habit of paying no attention to your instructions, you may have to practise some or all of the following in order to make sure s/he listens to what you ask him/her to do.

- Holding him/her still by the shoulders while you give the instruction.
- Looking right into his/her eyes.
- Talking in a clear and firm voice to him/her.
- Letting your face look stern while you speak.
- Having someone else around to back you up if the child ignores you.
- Insisting on being attended to and obeyed – for a reasonable instruction.

Things you can do when limits are ignored

Judicious ignoring

- Take absolutely no notice of swearing, rude remarks and protests.
- Ignore tantrums, shouts and screams by, whenever possible, leaving your child without an audience. Get on with your own affairs; for example, get out the Hoover so that the child's tantrums cannot be heard.
- If it really is important that s/he obeys you, show your child that you mean what you say; stand over him/her and repeat the instruction with a raised (*not* screaming) and firm voice, and also flashing eyes. **It is all right to look really angry!**

Giving instructions and commands

- Make commands short and to the point.
- Give one command at a time.
- Use commands that clearly specify the desired behaviour.
- Be realistic in your expectations and use age-appropriate commands.

- Don't use 'stop' commands; use 'do' commands.
- Make commands polite.
- Don't give unnecessary commands.
- Don't threaten children.
- Use 'when–then' commands ('*When* you've tidied up, *then* you can go out to play').
- Give children options whenever possible.
- Give children ample opportunity to comply.
- Praise compliance or provide consequences for noncompliance.
- Give warnings and helpful reminders.
- Support your partner's commands.
- Strike a balance between parental and child control.
- Encourage problem-solving with children.

Hints for Parents 3: Strengthening your child's self-control

Something worth remembering

Children whose parents set firm limits for them grow up with more self-esteem and confidence than those who are allowed to get away with behaving in any way they like, notably with aggression. It is important, however, to give youngsters some freedom of choice within reasonable limits.

Self-management training

There are techniques which can help to strengthen self-control. Training involves making your child aware of the circumstances in which s/he gets angry, and then moves through a series of stages. First, you would model the performance of a task, making appropriate and positive self-statements, such as 'Think first, act afterwards'; 'It's not worth losing my temper'; 'I'll count to ten and stay calm'. Your child then practises the same behaviour, gradually moving to whispered, and eventually silent, self-instruction. Children are encouraged to use these self-statements so that they can observe, evaluate and reinforce appropriate behaviour in themselves.

Logical consequences

If you ensure (within limits of safety) that your child is allowed to experience the consequences of his/her own actions, this becomes an effective means of modifying behaviour. If your child at mealtimes, say, throws food on the floor, s/he is more likely to learn to behave if s/he has to do without the meal. If you always replace the food s/he is likely to continue to be antisocial.

Unfortunately, from the point of view of the parents' self-interest, children are frequently not left to experience the consequences of their own misbehaviour. Against their own and the child's best interests parents intervene to protect their offspring from reality. The result, however, of this kindness or permissiveness is that the implications (outcomes) of the situation often do not become apparent to the child and they go on committing the same misdeeds over and over again. A good deal of thought is required here. To what extent (particularly with toddlers and teenagers) should you intervene (interfere?) to protect your child from the inevitable risks and knocks of life? To what extent is your child allowed to learn from experience – the hard way?